Jesus Calls

Scripture text from
The Contemporary English Version

- *The First Friends* — 2
- *The Twelve* — 8
- *Unwelcome* — 14
- *The Rich Young Man* — 20
- *A Demanding Road* — 26
- *At the Time of Jesus* — 32

AMERICAN
BIBLE
SOCIETY

CHAPTER 1
The First Friends

Fra Angelico
(1400-1455)
The Call of St. Peter and St. Andrew
Decorated letter from the Missal
(ms. 558 fol. 13v.)

Fra Angelico was a friar in Florence, Italy. He painted to decorate his convent and to help his fellow friars to pray. This illuminated letter O makes a perfect frame. What moment in the call of Peter and Andrew is he trying to imagine?

© Orsi Battaglini-Giraudon / San Marco Museum, Florence (Italy)

At the Lakeside

View of Nazareth

History

For 30 years Jesus lived in Nazareth. One day he decided to leave his family, his friends, and his village. Why? He knew that he was called to do God's work far beyond his own little village.

Almost 20 miles east of Nazareth are the clear waters of Lake Tiberias, teeming with fish. Jesus sees the fishermen busy with their boats and their nets, so he stops to speak with them.

He invites the fishermen to follow him and to share his work. The four men he calls are two sets of brothers from two different families: Simon and his brother Andrew, James and his brother John.

* **Lake Tiberias** *is also called the Lake of Gennesaret or the Sea of Galilee. It lies between the green hills of Galilee and the desert peaks of Syria, and is 13 miles long and seven and a half miles wide.*

Lake Tiberias

About Forty Years Later

Mark probably wrote his Gospel around A.D. 65 in Rome. At this time Simon (whom Jesus renamed Peter) and James had already been put to death for following Jesus. Mark had not been present at the lakeside, but it might have been Peter who told him how his first meeting with Jesus changed his life. Peter said that he had been a simple fisherman until Jesus invited him to become a "fisher of men and women."

A fisherman of Sri Lanka

Bible

Come with Me
Mark 1.14-20

After John was arrested, Jesus went to Galilee and told the good news that comes from God. He said, "The time has come! God's kingdom will soon be here. Turn back to God and believe the good news!"

As Jesus was walking along the shore of Lake Galilee, he saw Simon and his brother Andrew. They were fishermen and were casting their nets into the lake. Jesus said to them, "Come with me! I will teach you how to bring in people instead of fish." Right then the two brothers dropped their nets and went with him.

Kingdom of God

In Jesus' day this phrase made people think of a time when everyone would be happy and living by God's word. The Gospel does not explain the nature of the Kingdom (or Reign) of God. It describes the Kingdom. It is like a seed, like yeast. It has already begun, yet it is still to come in its fullness.

Good News

In Greek the word Gospel *(euag-gelion)* means "Good News." It is the announcement that God is coming to make people happy forever. Jesus announces the Good News to the poor. His apostles are sent to take this news to the whole world. The four Gospels (Matthew, Mark, Luke, and John) are books that tell the story of the Good News.

Zebedee

This name in Hebrew is pronounced "Zabday" and means "gift from God." In English we would say "God-given."

Today

The Call to His Followers

The Day Is Coming

The day is coming when you will have to leave your family, the close circle where you feel at home and loved. The day is coming when you will have to launch out and live your own life. The day is coming when you have to leave in order to create, to invent, to start things for yourself.

The Mission of Jesus

The day came when Jesus realized that he must leave his family and his village, to begin the mission his Father had entrusted to him: to proclaim God's love for everyone.

Call

When you need someone to undertake a special job, to carry out a mission, you "call" that person by name. "Come on…! I need you and your skills to share in this great mission. Are you willing to be part of it?"

Response

People who are called to a special task feel challenged. They may ask themselves "Can I do this? Is it really me you want?" Hopefully after they think about it, they will respond, "Well, if you have called me, here I am!"

Together

The work to which Jesus calls people is immense and challenging. It can seem overwhelming, but you are not called to work alone. All those who have been called can encourage and help one another. Everyone's efforts can be pooled together. Together their energy, their faith, and their enthusiasm have the strength to move mountains!

Those Who Say Yes

They are of all ages,
women, men and children.
They are from near and far:
workers, artists, students, the
unemployed, rich and poor, powerful
and ordinary.
They come from all corners of the
world to work together.

The call of Jesus has reached them,
touching their hearts and minds,
changing their lives.

They have decided to respond to
Jesus' call, to believe in him,
and to entrust themselves completely
to him.

They have decided
to follow Jesus Christ,
such as they are,
big or small, sinners or just,
brave or weak -
and to go with him,
no matter how difficult
the road may be,
to accomplish the mission
that Jesus entrusts to them:
to announce the love
of God
to the ends
of the earth!

CHAPTER 2

The Twelve

Fra Angelico
(1400-1455)
Sermon on the Mount
(after restoration)

Another Fra Angelico painting, but in a very different style from the one on page 2. Would you know it was by the same artist? Which painting might help you to pray?

© Orsi Battaglini - Giraudon / San Marco Museum, Florence (Italy)

History

They Followed Jesus

Sculpture of Peter in the church of St. Peter in Rome, Italy

Jesus did not work alone. He called a group of twelve, (the number of the twelve tribes of Israel), a number that signifies wholeness. These twelve disciples are called to stay with Jesus and then to be sent out. The leader of the group was probably Peter. Judas was in charge of the money. The twelve disciples stay with Jesus until his arrest.

The Twelve are not alone. There was a larger group of 72 followers who traveled with them. These followers are often forgotten. Among them, Jesus included a group of women. This would have been unusual at that time.*

The Work Continued

Jesus was betrayed by Judas, one of the Twelve. When Jesus was arrested all the other disciples kept their distance or ran away.

After the death and resurrection of Jesus, these disciples regained their courage. They came to understand in a new way what his presence ("being with him") and mission ("being sent by him") meant. They were to carry the Good News all the way to the very ends of the earth.

The enthusiasm of the newest apostles, like Paul, encouraged the disciples to be even bolder in proclaiming the Good News. The women played an important role in welcoming groups of Christians to their homes. When the Christian communities retold the story of the call of the Twelve, they could see that they too were continuing the mission for which the Twelve had been prepared.

Statue of Mary Magdalene at Lestelle-Betharam in France

* Among the women who followed Jesus and are mentioned in the Gospels were "Mary Magdalene... Joanna, Susanna and many others" (Luke 8.2,3), "Jesus' mother... with her sister" (John 19.25), and "many women had come with Jesus from Galilee... Mary, the mother of James and Joseph, and the mother of James and John." (Matthew 27.55,56).

Bible

He Calls the Twelve
Mark 3.13-19

Jesus decided to ask some of his disciples to go up on a mountain with him, and they went. Then he chose twelve of them to be his apostles, so that they could be with him. He also wanted to send them out to preach and to force out demons. Simon was one of the twelve, and Jesus named him Peter. There were also James and John, the two sons of Zebedee. Jesus called them Boanerges, which means "Thunderbolts." Andrew, Philip, Bartholomew, Matthew, Thomas, James son of Alphaeus, and Thaddaeus were also apostles. The others were Simon, known as the Eager One, and Judas Iscariot, who later betrayed Jesus.

What Do the Names of the Twelve Apostles Mean?

Simon: God has answered
Peter: Rock
John: God has graced
James: He will take charge
Andrew: Courageous
Philip: Lover of horses
Bartholomew: Son of Ptolomy
Matthew: Gift of God
Thomas: Twin
James, son of Alphaeus: James, son of the cattle farmer
Thaddeus (Jude): Gift of God
Simon the Patriot: Simon the freedom-fighter
Judas Iscariot: The man from Kariot, the land of ravines, (near Hebron)

Why Twelve?

Twelve is not just a number selected by chance. It has a deep meaning. It is used to symbolize completeness. There were twelve tribes in Israel. There are twelve months in the year. Jesus chose twelve disciples.

Today

Mission

Team...
It is impossible to succeed in any big project without gathering and working with a team. The team members put into practice the plans that had been already been decided. They dedicate themselves completely to the work.

...variety
The strength of a team and its ability to be creative come from its different members. Different ideas are needed: different characters, different minds, backgrounds, ways of going about things. The skills of each person will help the task to be completed.

Unique
Each person has a special place on the team. A person's talent, their know-how, makes that person irreplaceable and unique. In a team each person plays a particular part which no one else can play.

Mission
The team gathered together by Jesus is made up of all those who answer his call and who put his word into practice. To that team — the Church — Jesus entrusts the mission of proclaiming the Good News of God's love.

Apostles and Disciples
Everyone is called to be an apostle, that is, someone who is sent, a messenger. All people, with their gifts of body and spirit, are called by Jesus to his apostles, his envoys, his messengers who are sent to make God's love visible for everyone.

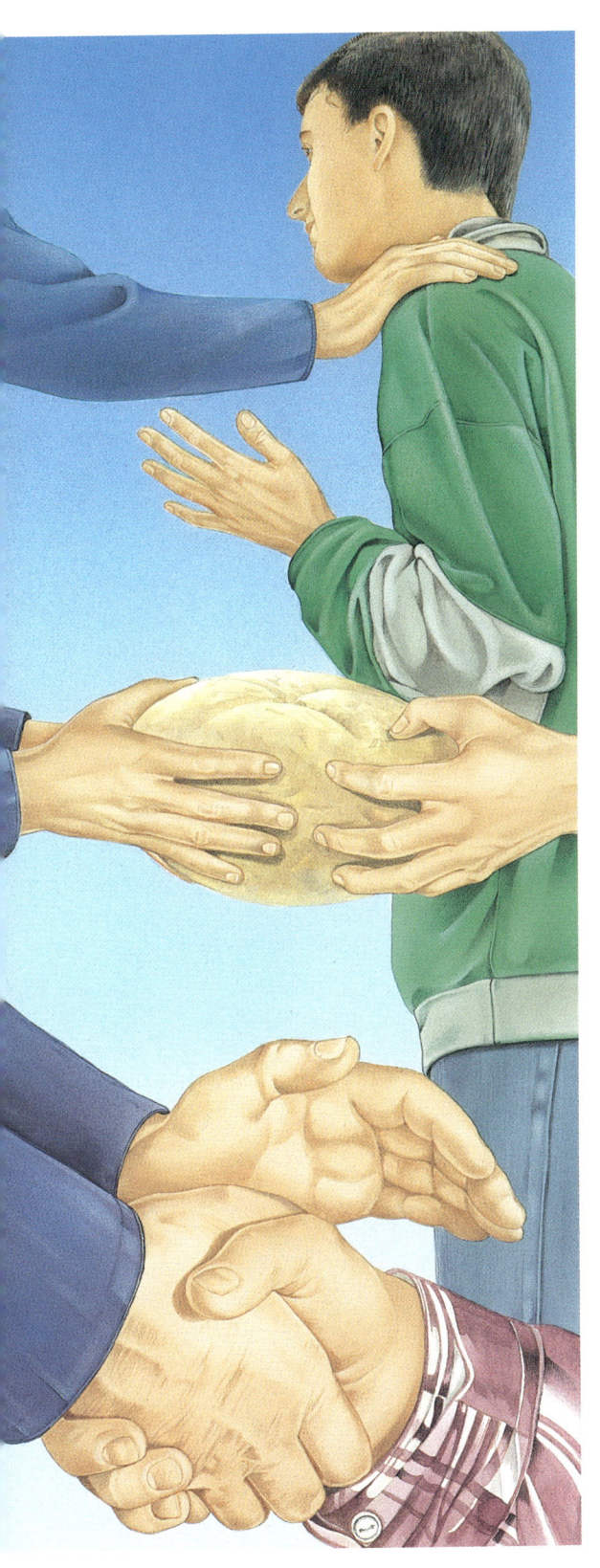

Still Counting!

How many apostles !
All over the world
they are answering Jesus' call.

What do they do today?
They forgive those who do wrong.
They reveal the power of gentleness.
They love God and their neighbors
with a love that
overcomes everything.

What do they do today?
They hold out healing hands.
They remove the poison of jealousy.
They break bread together.
They pray to their Father in heaven
and offer happiness to all
God's children on earth.

Would you like to add your name
to the long list of today's
apostles?

CHAPTER · 3

Unwelcome

Paolo Caliari, also known as **Veronese** (1528-1588), *The Banquet at Levi's House*

The artist has pictured Levi's dinner party in the richness of his own century. All the characters in the painting seem to have lots to attract their attention, but at the center of all this Jesus and Levi are deep in conversation.

© Giraudon - Private Collection, Paris (France)

It's a Scandal!

Customs officers and tax collectors (often called publicans) were very unpopular in early Israel. People accused them of getting rich illegally, of demanding more in taxes than the State required, and of then keeping the extra for themselves. The Pharisees blamed them for having contact with the pagans and so making themselves ritually impure. The tax collectors were considered sinners.

Jesus' behavior was surprising. He called a customs officer – a tax collector – Levi, son of Alphaeus, to follow him. Levi organised a meal at home with his publican friends, and he invited Jesus and his disciples to eat with them. The leaders of the Pharisees said it was a scandal: "You don't eat with that sort of people!" Jesus explains his action: "I have not come to call good people, but sinners."

History

A woman making bread in Egypt

A Real Welcome

Harvest of tea leaves in Sri Lanka

After the death and resurrection of Jesus, Christians used to come together to eat, to pray, and to remember Jesus. Soon problems arose. The rich took the best places, and the poor were left to one side. Some Jewish Christians refused to share the meal with non-Jewish Christians.

The example of Jesus, who ate with publicans and sinners, helped the first Christians to understand that they were called to welcome everybody around the same table.

In God's sight, people are neither Jew nor pagan, slave nor free.

A villager offering bread in Romania

* The people of Jesus' time had to pay many taxes. To the Roman empire they paid land tax, people tax, road tax, and taxes on bridges and markets. The publicans were in charge of collecting this money. Besides this, the Jews paid a Temple tax and tithes (a tenth) on the land and any produce which they grew.

Bible

Jesus and Levi

Mark 2.13-17

Once again, Jesus went to the shore of Lake Galilee. A large crowd gathered around him, and he taught them. As he walked along, he saw Levi, the son of Alphaeus. Levi was sitting at the place for paying taxes, and Jesus said to him, "Come with me!" So he got up and went with Jesus.

Later, Jesus and his disciples were having dinner at Levi's house. Many tax collectors and other sinners had become followers of Jesus, and they were also guests at the dinner.

Some of the teachers of the Law of Moses were Pharisees, and they saw that Jesus was eating with sinners and tax collectors. So they asked his disciples, "Why does he eat with tax collectors and sinners?"

Jesus heard them and answered, "Healthy people don't need a doctor, but sick people do. I didn't come to invite good people to be my followers. I came to invite sinners."

Levi

The "Levi" of the Scripture text is probably "Matthew the tax collector" (Matthew 10.3), the author of the Gospel that bears his name.

"Follow me!"

In the Gospels, the phrase "to follow someone" does not just mean "to walk behind someone." To follow Jesus means to be close to him, to share his life and deeds, to believe in him, and to be ready to give your life for him.

Pharisees

The Pharisees were completely dedicated to the Law of Moses. They wanted to make every one of its laws applicable to everyday life. The Gospels often showed them to be hypocrites.

Today

A Chance for Everyone

Goodness

No one, except Jesus Christ is without sin. Being good means trying to follow the example of Jesus, loving God as a Father and our neighbors as brothers and sisters.

Sinner

Everyone is a sinner because we all give in to evil and do wrong sometimes. But no one needs to remain trapped in the power of sin forever. To be a sinner means turning away from the example of Jesus and living far from the love of God and neighbor.

Labels

It is easy to label people "good" or "evil." Aren't we all sometimes good and sometimes bad?

Change

Just because people may do wrong does not mean that they should be considered bad forever! Everyone, with God's help, is capable of change, of turning back. When evil appears attractive, we can, with God's help, choose to say "no" and turn away.

Not Rejected But Loved

Jesus rejects no one. He calls each person to turn from wrong and respond to his love. For God the Father, there is no such thing as a hated sinner. They are just children for whom God cares very much.

All Alike

Alike!
We are all the same.

One day
full of generosity
giving without counting,
and the next day
fired up with temper
and full of anger!

One day
my lips bear
the sun's own smile,
and then on another day
my mouth spits out
mocking words
which slice deeper than a knife.

All alike:
we are good
and we are sinners!

God trusts everyone.
God trusts me
and never stops giving me
the chance
to live in the light,
of God's love
and truth!

CHAPTER 4
The Rich Young Man

Painted mural of Christ in the monastery of Eski Gümüs, Turkey

Can you imagine looking up at this painting high on the dome or wall of a great church? How different is it from paintings or statues of Jesus in churches you know?

© F. Zvardon

A Newcomer

History

A young Palestinian on a donkey

Lots of people were following Jesus. Some had left everything to be with him. Peter, Andrew, and John left their fishing business. Levi abandoned his work as a tax collector. Others traveled great distances from their homes, their families, and their villages. Some were poor with no possessions, jobs, or families.

One day a young man rushed up to Jesus and said, "What must I do to gain eternal life?" When he told Jesus that he was already obeying the commandments of the Law of Moses, Jesus suggested he could do more. "Sell your possessions and give the money to the poor!" The young man bowed his head to the ground and went off sad. He was too attached to his wealth.

Statue in the Israel Museum in Jerusalem

The First Christians and the Poor

Mark told this story to the rich and the poor Christians in his community. What is the point of the story?
- That Jesus loves them too, just as he loved the man who rushed up to him.
- That Jesus is asking them to keep the commandments and suggesting that they go farther.
- Some Christians had already sold their goods and shared the money with the poor.* The joy of sharing is worth more than the sadness of everyone looking after him or herself.

Carrying bricks in Nepal

* The Acts of the Apostles, which recounts the life of the first Christians and the growth of the Church, says, "All the Lord's followers often met together, and they shared everything they had." (Acts 2.44)

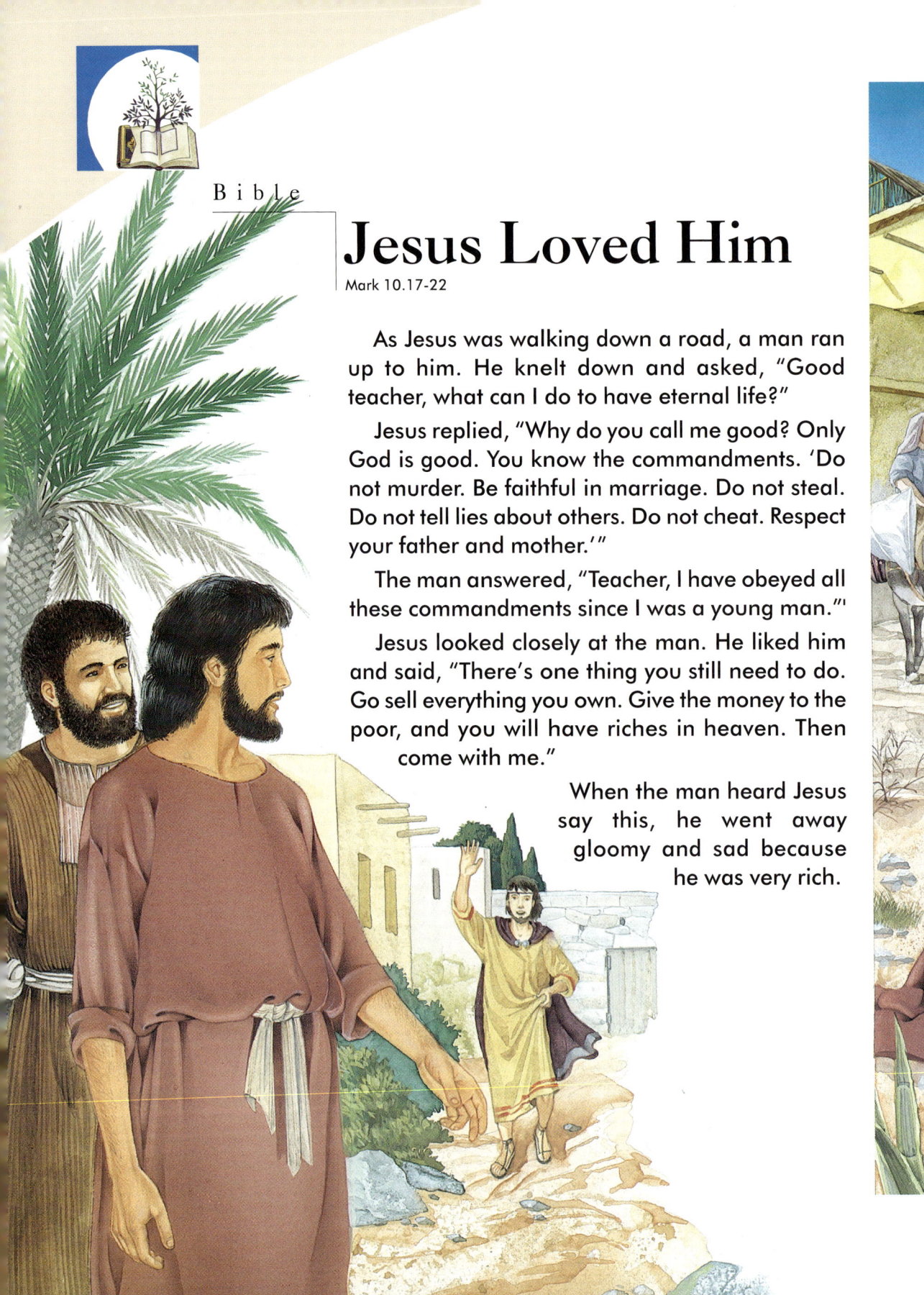

Bible

Jesus Loved Him
Mark 10.17-22

As Jesus was walking down a road, a man ran up to him. He knelt down and asked, "Good teacher, what can I do to have eternal life?"

Jesus replied, "Why do you call me good? Only God is good. You know the commandments. 'Do not murder. Be faithful in marriage. Do not steal. Do not tell lies about others. Do not cheat. Respect your father and mother.'"

The man answered, "Teacher, I have obeyed all these commandments since I was a young man."'

Jesus looked closely at the man. He liked him and said, "There's one thing you still need to do. Go sell everything you own. Give the money to the poor, and you will have riches in heaven. Then come with me."

When the man heard Jesus say this, he went away gloomy and sad because he was very rich.

Good Teacher

The young man addressed Jesus as "good." Jesus reminded him that it is only God who is to be called "good."

Commandments

The Ten Commandments are the heart of the Law of Moses which faithful Jews observe.

Decisions

The young man went away. Jesus never forces anyone. People are free to follow him or to go their own way.

Today

Difficult Decisions

Riches

We are rich if we have all we wish for and do not have to worry about tomorrow. We are rich if we have the chance to meet people, to have friends and be loved, to have many skills and develop our qualities. To be rich is not a bad thing. It is a great responsibility.

Attached to Wealth

Jesus does not reject rich people. He never rejects anyone! He simply warns them of the danger of ending up prisoners of the wealth they possess.

What might be holding us prisoner?

To Follow Jesus...

How can we truly follow Jesus if we are imprisoned in any way?

Wholeheartedly

The road of love that people take with Jesus asks them to give more than just a little and more than just for a short time. On that road people share; they do not just look after themselves. On that road with Jesus, people do not just give a bit, they give wholeheartedly!

Free To Choose

Jesus leaves everyone free to choose, to accept or refuse to go farther, to share or to keep selfishly. But whatever decision a person makes, Christ's love for that person remains unchanged.

Treasures

What priceless treasures
you possess:
the goodness of your heart,
the joy of your smile,
the skills of your hands
and your intelligence!
Will you share them generously?

What riches you possess!

What about the words
from your lips!
Will you use them
to defend those
who are persecuted?

What about the strength
of your courage!
Will you use it to lift up
those who fall
under the weight of sorrow?

What about the happiness
of your life!
Will you use it
to surround with light
those who lose their way
in the night of worry?

What treasures you have!
Will you offer them
in following
Christ Jesus?

CHAPTER 5

A Demanding Road

Decorated letter *D* from the Missal: Entrance into Jerusalem, c. 1500

Another example of an illuminated letter from a prayer book. This is from the sixteenth century. There is much more detail than in the O on page 2. What event in the life of Jesus is pictured here?

© Bridgeman-Giraudon / Wallace Collection, London (England)

Knowing Where You Are Going

History

The Coliseum in Rome, Italy

People followed Jesus for various reasons. Some people thought he would overthrow the Romans.* They were hoping for a good place in the Kingdom that Jesus proclaimed. Jesus did not mislead them. He told them that it would not always be easy, and they would have to carry the cross daily.

Jesus prepared to go up to Jerusalem, where he would face the civil and religious leaders. These people did not agree with his message. To go up to Jerusalem was to risk his life. Eventually he would be crucified. Will those who have begun to answer his call follow him right to the end?

Remembering the Words of Jesus

There are some words which renew our courage. A long time later, when the early Christians read the words of Jesus in Luke's Gospel, they had a better understanding of the difficulties they faced because of Jesus' message – separation from their family, having to travel to spread the Good News, and the problems of daily life.

Statue of a Roman soldier on the Victor Emmanuel Bridge in Rome, Italy

Bridge in Carpates, Romania

> *At the time of Jesus, his country was occupied by Roman armies. Pontius Pilate, a representative of the emperor, controlled the country. Many people in Jesus' day were hoping to be set free.

Bible

Carrying Your Cross

Luke 9.57-61, 23

Along the way someone said to Jesus, "I'll go anywhere with you!"

Jesus said, "Foxes have dens, and birds have nests, but the Son of Man doesn't have a place to call his own."

Jesus told someone else to come with him. But the man said, "Lord, let me wait until I bury my father."

Jesus answered, "Let the dead take care of the dead, while you go and tell about God's kingdom."

Then someone said to Jesus, "I want to go with you, Lord, but first let me go back and take care of things at home."

Then Jesus said to all the people:

"If any of you want to be my followers, you must forget about yourself. You must take up your cross each day and follow me."

On the Road

After leaving his village of Nazareth, Jesus traveled all around the country. He was always on the road. When people heard his words and saw what he did, many of them wanted to follow him.

Son of Man

This phrase recalls a vision from the prophet Daniel (about 175 B.C.). He describes the coming of a "Son of Man" on the clouds of heaven to save his people from judgment. The first Christians believed that Jesus is the Son of Man who was to come at the end of time.

Cross

The cross was seen as an instrument of terrible and humiliating torture. From the start, many could not understand Jesus' crucifixion. Gradually the followers of Jesus understood that like him, they too had to "carry their cross" – accept the hard things in their life, each and every day.

Today

The Way of Jesus

Leader

Jesus is not just a revolutionary or a philosopher with new ideas. Nor is he a teacher thinking up interesting theories.

Jesus is the Savior coming to free people from all that imprisons them. Jesus is the Son of God coming to teach people to live with a love for God and for their neighbors.

Life's Road...

Those who decide to follow Jesus choose a path that will change their lives.

Jesus leads them along a road where they will share with each other, give to one another, and believe in God and in each other.

... a Difficult Road

The road to which Jesus calls his friends is hard. Jesus asks them to give up being self-centered, to leave pride behind, to stop being small minded, to carry the burden of others, to believe in him without seeing him.

... a New Road

The road to which Jesus calls is completely new! It is a road where you pray for your enemies, where you always forgive a person who wrongs you, where you share without counting the cost, where you trust and place yourself completely in the hands of God.

... of Love

Jesus calls us to love ! Nothing less! Jesus proclaims and shows people that only love is able to transform the world into a kingdom where all are equal children of God.

On the Way

They set out on the road
with the unforgettable
words of Jesus
singing in their hearts
and in their lives.

They set out,
opening their arms
to those who are wounded
by daily worries and fears.
They set out to offer
the daily gift of kindness.

The unforgettable words of Jesus,
burn like flames of fire in their memory.
And these words are a daily call,
urging them to continue on earth
the work of love and of peace,
which the Lord Jesus began
when he gave his life
to save the world!

INSIGHTS

At the Time of Jesus

The Country (see map on page 35)

The land where Jesus walked is a small, rather poor country. From Nazareth to Jerusalem it is only about 70 miles. The country had been occupied by Roman troops since 63 B.C. It is a land with a long and difficult history, a place from where all points of the world and all kinds of people could be reached.

The Regions

In the north, *Galilee* has a pleasant climate, with charming villages and a clear lake. In the center is the hilly region of *Samaria*. The inhabitants of this region, the Samaritans, are despised by their neighbors. In the south is *Judea,* a mountainous region, partly desert country with a harsh climate.

Jerusalem, the ruins of a synagogue

The Towns

The Roman and Jewish authorities have their headquarters in *Jerusalem,* the capital city. It is also the religious center of the country because the Temple is there. Jesus was crucified in *Jerusalem. Bethlehem,* the hometown of King David, is also the birthplace of Jesus as told in the Gospels. Yet Jesus spent the largest part of his life in *Nazareth,* a little village in *Galilee.* He began his public ministry in the Capernaum area, the town of the apostle Peter.

The Judean countryside

Geography

To the west lay the Mediterranean Sea, often called the *Great Sea*. To the east, the *Jordan River* flows in a deep valley through *Lake Tiberias* and south toward the *Dead Sea*, which in Jesus' day was called the *Salt Sea*.

The country can be divided into four strips, each parallel to the sea.

1. A coastal plain narrowing toward the north.
2. A mountain chain where some peaks are over 3,000 feet high. It is desert-like in the south, with rich valleys in the north.
3. The deepest trench in the world, the Jordan Valley. The surface of the Dead Sea is about 1,300 feet below sea level.
4. Various plateaus beyond the Jordan. Certain peaks are more than 4,000 feet high.

Today

The largest part of the country where Jesus lived now belongs to *Israel* and contains territories inhabited and governed by *Palestinians*. The neighboring countries are Lebanon to the north, Syria and Jordan to the east, and Egypt to the south.

Lake Tiberias

Titles already published:

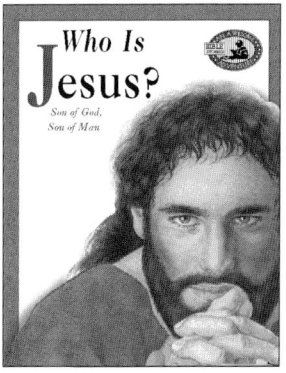

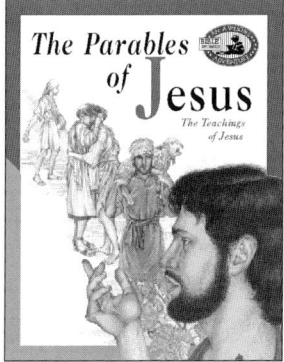

Forthcoming titles in the JUNIOR BIBLE Collection:

- The First Prophets
- Passion and Resurrection
- Exile and Return
- Isaiah, Micah, Jeremiah
- Jesus and the Outcasts
- Jesus in Jerusalem
- Acts
- Wisdom
- Psalms
- Women
- Revelation
- Letters

Jesus Calls

Vol. 8

This is a Portion of Holy Scripture in the *Contemporary English Version*. The American Bible Society is a not-for-profit organization which publishes the Scriptures without doctrinal note or comment. Since 1816, its single mission has been to make the Word of God easily available to people everywhere at the lowest possible cost and in the languages they understand best. Working toward this goal, the ABS is a member of the United Bible Societies, a worldwide effort that extends to more than 180 countries and territories. You are urged to read the Bible and to share it with others. For a catalog of other Scripture publications, call us toll-free at 1-800-32 BIBLE, or write to the American Bible Society, 1865 Broadway, New York, NY 10023. Visit our website: www.americanbible.org

© 1998 ÉDITIONS DU SIGNE

Original text by: Liam KELLY, Anne WHITE, Albert HARI, Charles SINGER
English text adapted by: The American Bible Society
Photography: Frantisek ZVARDON
Illustrators: Mariano VALSESIA, Betti FERRERO MIA. Milan Illustrations Agency
Layout: Bayle Graphic Studio

ISBN 1-58516-136-5
Printed in Italy - Stige, Torino
Eng. Port. CEV 560 P - 109854
ABS 8-9/00

Scripture text
CEV Copyright
© 1995, American Bible Society